Marco and ... to Play Ball

A True Story Promoting Inclusion and Self-Determination

Finding My Way Series

Jo Meserve Mach
Vera Lynne Stroup-Rentier

Photography by Mary Birdsell

BROWN BOOKS
PUBLISHING GROUP

Marco and I Want to Play Ball.
A True Story Promoting Inclusion and Self-Determination

Brown Books Kids
16250 Knoll Trail Drive, Suite 205
Dallas, Texas 75248
www.BrownBooksKids.com
(972) 381-0009

A New Era in Publishing®

ISBN 978-1-61254-257-7
LCCN 2016913962

Printed in the United States
10 9 8 7 6 5 4 3 2 1

For more information or to contact the author, please go to
www.findingmywaybooks.com

Hi, my name is Isiah.
My cousin, Marco, and I love to play ball.

We like to play ball with Grandpa.
He makes playing ball super fun.

"Play ball, Grandpa?"
Grandpa shakes his head.
He's tired.

We hear Grandpa snoring.
Marco and I want to play ball outside.

At last we hear him say, "Let's play ball, boys."

Marco yells, "My ball is going to hit the barn."
"No, it won't," I yell back.

Marco swings and misses.
Grandpa tells Marco to watch the ball.

Marco hits a fly ball.
"I can hit one higher," I yell.
"No, you can't," yells Marco.

Marco swings and misses.
Marco swings again.
Marco slams it right to me.
"Good hit, Marco."

I'm coming in to bat.

First, we help Grandpa pick up balls.

"Batter up," says Grandpa.

"I'm going to hit the barn," I yell.
"No you're not," Marco yells back.

The ball hits the swing set.
"That's not the barn," laughs Marco.

I swing and miss.
Grandpa tells me to hold my elbow up.

I have a good hit.

Is Marco going to catch it?

"Good catch, Marco."

It's my turn to catch.
"This time I'm going to hit the barn,"
says Marco.
"No, you won't," I tell him.

Grandpa tells Marco to stand tall.
Marco hits the ball as hard as he can.

Wow! The ball is stuck in a tree.
"That's not the barn," I laugh.
Marco laughs too.

Marco and I can get the ball.

"Good job, boys," says Grandpa.
"It's the last round.
You each get too more hits."

Marco hits the ball high.
"I almost hit the barn," yells Marco.
"No, you didn't," I yell back.
Marco hits the ball low.

It's my turn to bat.
I swing and miss.

I swing and miss again!
Grandpa tells me not to throw the bat.

Marco yells, "You can do it, Isiah."
I stand tall.
I watch the ball.
I hold my elbow up.

I hit the ball as hard as I can.
Wow!

I did it!
I hit the barn!

We have so much fun playing ball
with Grandpa.